Go Fish

FISHING JOURNAL

ARTWORK BY

JAMES PROSEK

Stewart, Tabori & Chang
New York

Published in 2000 by
Stewart, Tabori & Chang
A division of U.S. Media Holdings, Inc.
115 West 18th Street
New York, NY 10011

Distributed in Canada by
General Publishing Company Ltd.
30 Lesmill Road
Don Mills, Ontario, Canada M3B 2T6

ISBN: 1-58479-017-2

Printed in Singapore

10 9 8 7 6 5 4 3 2 1

First Printing

Front cover designed by John Gray and Nina Barnett

Designed by Nina Barnett

Edited by Julie Ho

Production by Kim Tyner

The text for this journal was composed in New Baskerville

Printed in Singapore by Tien Wah Press

FRONT COVER:

Brown Trout with Rod, *from the private collection of*
Marie and Bill Pastore

PAGE 3:

Brown trout chasing a fly under the butterburr,
River Dove, England

PAGE 4:

Brown trout in the River Test, England

PAGE 133:

Male and female brook trout on a bed of moss

PAGE 134:

Bluefish in the Race, near Watch Hill, Rhode Island

Go Fish: Fishing Journal features portraits of fish from acclaimed author and painter James Prosek.
Several of these fish were caught on Prosek's recent travels on the 41st latitude; he is fishing around the world
and researching material for his next book. Hailed as the "Audubon of the fishing world" by *The New York Times*
for his debut book of watercolor portraits of trout, Prosek is the author of *Trout, Joe and Me,*
The Complete Angler, and *Early Love and Brook Trout.* A graduate of Yale University, he lives in Connecticut.

Visit his official website www.troutsite.com
.

DATE

TIME

LOCATION

WEATHER

WATER

ROD & REEL

FLY

FISH

SIZE & WEIGHT

DATE

TIME

LOCATION

WEATHER

WATER

ROD & REEL

FLY

FISH

SIZE & WEIGHT

DATE

TIME

LOCATION

WEATHER

WATER

ROD & REEL

FLY

FISH

SIZE & WEIGHT

DATE

TIME

LOCATION

WEATHER

WATER

ROD & REEL

FLY

FISH

SIZE & WEIGHT

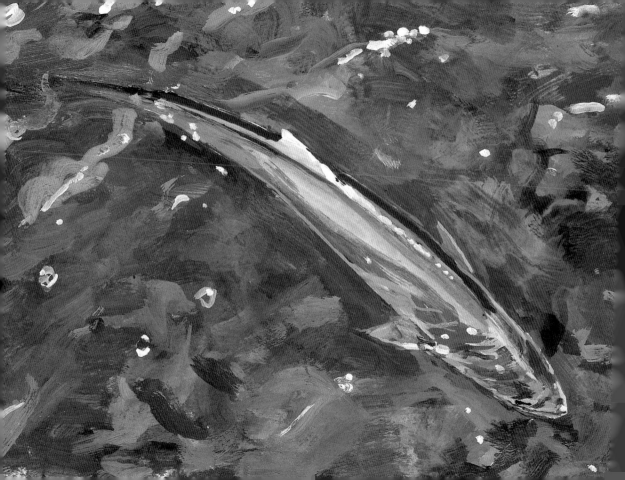

DATE

TIME

LOCATION

WEATHER

WATER

ROD & REEL

FLY

FISH

SIZE & WEIGHT

DATE

TIME

LOCATION

WEATHER

WATER

ROD & REEL

FLY

FISH

SIZE & WEIGHT

DATE

TIME

LOCATION

WEATHER

WATER

ROD & REEL

FLY

FISH

SIZE & WEIGHT

DATE

TIME

LOCATION

WEATHER

WATER

ROD & REEL

FLY

FISH

SIZE & WEIGHT

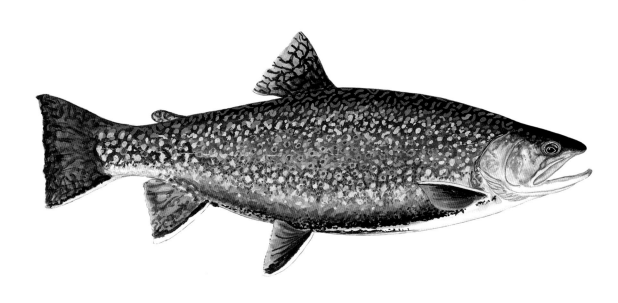

Labrador brook trout from Minipi Lake, Labrador, Canada

Brook trout from Lac Doigt D'or, Quebec

DATE

TIME

LOCATION

WEATHER

WATER

ROD & REEL

FLY

FISH

SIZE & WEIGHT

DATE

TIME

LOCATION

WEATHER

WATER

ROD & REEL

FLY

FISH

SIZE & WEIGHT

DATE

TIME

LOCATION

WEATHER

WATER

ROD & REEL

FLY

FISH

SIZE & WEIGHT

DATE

TIME

LOCATION

WEATHER

WATER

ROD & REEL

FLY

FISH

SIZE & WEIGHT

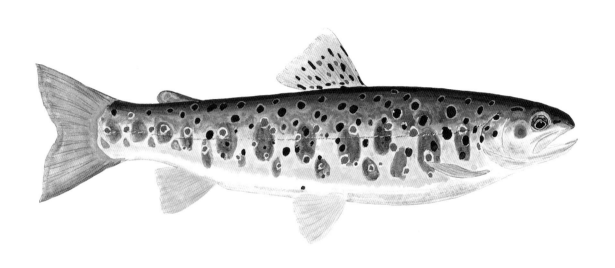

Brown trout from Manastir Brook, western Turkey

Softmouth trout from Krka River, Croatia

DATE

TIME

LOCATION

WEATHER

WATER

ROD & REEL

FLY

FISH

SIZE & WEIGHT

NOTES

DATE

TIME

LOCATION

WEATHER

WATER

ROD & REEL

FLY

FISH

SIZE & WEIGHT

DATE

TIME

LOCATION

WEATHER

WATER

ROD & REEL

FLY

FISH

SIZE & WEIGHT

DATE

TIME

LOCATION

WEATHER

WATER

ROD & REEL

FLY

FISH

SIZE & WEIGHT

White-spotted char, upper tributary of Kiso River, Japan

Brown trout from small mountain stream,
Slovenia

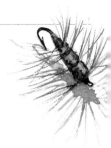

DATE

TIME

LOCATION

WEATHER

WATER

ROD & REEL

FLY

FISH

SIZE & WEIGHT

DATE

TIME

LOCATION

WEATHER

WATER

ROD & REEL

FLY

FISH

SIZE & WEIGHT

DATE

TIME

LOCATION

WEATHER

WATER

ROD & REEL

FLY

FISH

SIZE & WEIGHT

DATE

TIME

LOCATION

WEATHER

WATER

ROD & REEL

FLY

FISH

SIZE & WEIGHT

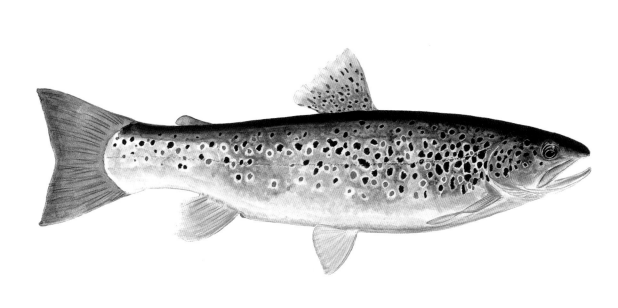

Brown trout from Voidomatis River,
northwest Greece

Brook trout from a dark tannic stream, Connecticut

NOTES

DATE

TIME

LOCATION

WEATHER

WATER

ROD & REEL

FLY

FISH

SIZE & WEIGHT

DATE

TIME

LOCATION

WEATHER

WATER

ROD & REEL

FLY

FISH

SIZE & WEIGHT

DATE

TIME

LOCATION

WEATHER

WATER

ROD & REEL

FLY

FISH

SIZE & WEIGHT

DATE

TIME

LOCATION

WEATHER

WATER

ROD & REEL

FLY

FISH

SIZE & WEIGHT

Brook trout from Appalachian Mountain stream, Georgia

Flat-headed trout from Zamanti River, central Turkey

DATE

TIME

LOCATION

WEATHER

WATER

ROD & REEL

FLY

FISH

SIZE & WEIGHT

DATE

TIME

LOCATION

WEATHER

WATER

ROD & REEL

FLY

FISH

SIZE & WEIGHT

DATE

TIME

LOCATION

WEATHER

WATER

ROD & REEL

FLY

FISH

SIZE & WEIGHT

DATE

TIME

LOCATION

WEATHER

WATER

ROD & REEL

FLY

FISH

SIZE & WEIGHT

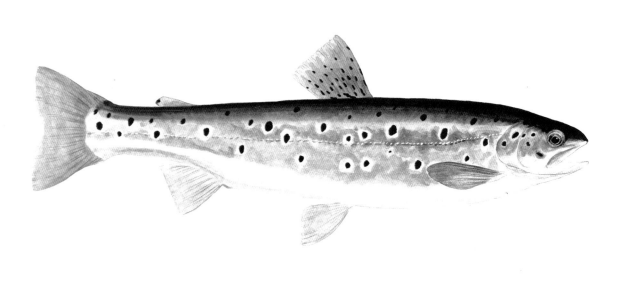

Brown trout from Balik Lake, eastern Turkey

Arctic char from Chukotka River, Russia

DATE

TIME

LOCATION

WEATHER

WATER

ROD & REEL

FLY

FISH

SIZE & WEIGHT

DATE

TIME

LOCATION

WEATHER

WATER

ROD & REEL

FLY

FISH

SIZE & WEIGHT

DATE

TIME

LOCATION

WEATHER

WATER

ROD & REEL

FLY

FISH

SIZE & WEIGHT

DATE

TIME

LOCATION

WEATHER

WATER

ROD & REEL

FLY

FISH

SIZE & WEIGHT

Softmouth trout from Buna River, Bosnia

Smallmouth bass from Candlewood Lake, Connecticut

DATE

TIME

LOCATION

WEATHER

WATER

ROD & REEL

FLY

FISH

SIZE & WEIGHT

DATE

TIME

LOCATION

WEATHER

WATER

ROD & REEL

FLY

FISH

SIZE & WEIGHT

DATE

TIME

LOCATION

WEATHER

WATER

ROD & REEL

FLY

FISH

SIZE & WEIGHT

DATE

TIME

LOCATION

WEATHER

WATER

ROD & REEL

FLY

FISH

SIZE & WEIGHT

Arctic char from a Scottish lake

Atlantic salmon from Bonaventure River, Gaspé, Quebec

DATE

TIME

LOCATION

WEATHER

WATER

ROD & REEL

FLY

FISH

SIZE & WEIGHT

DATE

TIME

LOCATION

WEATHER

WATER

ROD & REEL

FLY

FISH

SIZE & WEIGHT

DATE

TIME

LOCATION

WEATHER

WATER

ROD & REEL

FLY

FISH

SIZE & WEIGHT

DATE

TIME

LOCATION

WEATHER

WATER

ROD & REEL

FLY

FISH

SIZE & WEIGHT

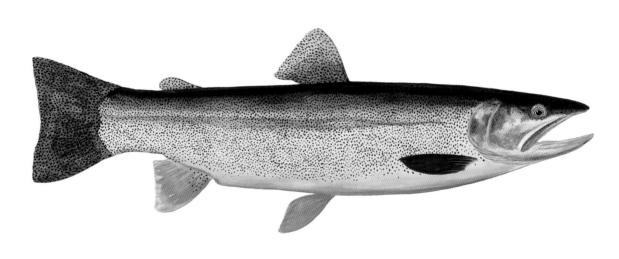

Snake River fine-spotted cutthroat trout from Gros Ventre River,
Jackson Hole, Wyoming

Southern Appalachia brook trout from
a small stream in the Hiwassee River drainage,
Smoky Mountains, Tennessee

DATE

TIME

LOCATION

WEATHER

WATER

ROD & REEL

FLY

FISH

SIZE & WEIGHT

DATE

TIME

LOCATION

WEATHER

WATER

ROD & REEL

FLY

FISH

SIZE & WEIGHT

DATE

TIME

LOCATION

WEATHER

WATER

ROD & REEL

FLY

FISH

SIZE & WEIGHT

DATE

TIME

LOCATION

WEATHER

WATER

ROD & REEL

FLY

FISH

SIZE & WEIGHT

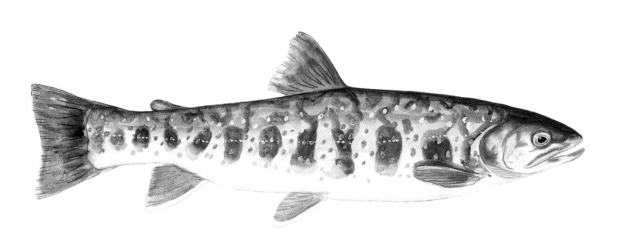

Dolly Varden trout, resident male spawner,
from Chukotka River, Russia

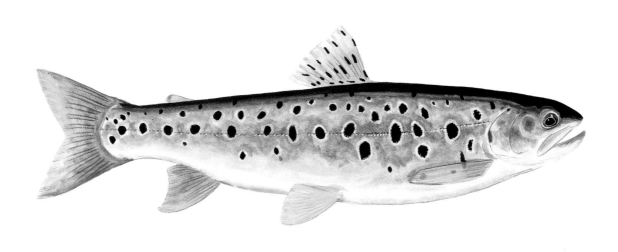

Brown trout from Lake Abant, Turkey

DATE

TIME

LOCATION

WEATHER

WATER

ROD & REEL

FLY

FISH

SIZE & WEIGHT

NOTES

DATE

TIME

LOCATION

WEATHER

WATER

ROD & REEL

FLY

FISH

SIZE & WEIGHT

DATE

TIME

LOCATION

WEATHER

WATER

ROD & REEL

FLY

FISH

SIZE & WEIGHT

DATE

TIME

LOCATION

WEATHER

WATER

ROD & REEL

FLY

FISH

SIZE & WEIGHT

Marble trout from Soca River, Slovenia

Brown trout from Krka River, Croatia

DATE

TIME

LOCATION

WEATHER

WATER

ROD & REEL

FLY

FISH

SIZE & WEIGHT

NOTES

DATE

TIME

LOCATION

WEATHER

WATER

ROD & REEL

FLY

FISH

SIZE & WEIGHT

DATE

TIME

LOCATION

WEATHER

WATER

ROD & REEL

FLY

FISH

SIZE & WEIGHT

DATE

TIME

LOCATION

WEATHER

WATER

ROD & REEL

FLY

FISH

SIZE & WEIGHT

Yellowstone cutthroat trout from Yellowstone River,
Buffalo Ford, Wyoming

Brown trout from an Irish lake

DATE

TIME

LOCATION

WEATHER

WATER

ROD & REEL

FLY

FISH

SIZE & WEIGHT

DATE

TIME

LOCATION

WEATHER

WATER

ROD & REEL

FLY

FISH

SIZE & WEIGHT

DATE

TIME

LOCATION

WEATHER

WATER

ROD & REEL

FLY

FISH

SIZE & WEIGHT

DATE

TIME

LOCATION

WEATHER

WATER

ROD & REEL

FLY

FISH

SIZE & WEIGHT